Where Are You Going?

Written by Art Sipowitz
Illustrated by Fraser Williamson

Aquarium

Palac

I am going
to the aquarium.

I am going
to the palace.

I am going
to the lake.

I am going
to the river.

I am going
to the park.

I am going to the store.

I am going
to the moon.

8